Contents

Smarter than people?

Machines can't think like people.
But some machines are very clever.
Inventors create machines to do jobs
that people can't do. Some smart
machines help us do very difficult
or dangerous jobs.

EXTREME MACHINES

THE WORLD'S SMARTEST MACHINES

Linda Tagliaferro

www.raintreepublishers.co.uk
Visit our website to find out more information about Raintree books.

To order:
☎ Phone 0845 6044371
🖷 Fax +44 (0) 1865 312263
🖳 Email myorders@raintreepublishers.co.uk

Customers from outside the UK please telephone +44 1865 312262

Raintree is an imprint of Capstone Global Library Limited, a company incorporated in England and Wales having its registered office at 7 Pilgrim Street, London, EC4V 6LB – Registered company number: 6695582

Edited by Nancy Dickmann and Megan Cotugno
Designed by Jo Hinton-Malivoire
Picture research by Tracy Cummins
Originated by Capstone Global Library
Printed and bound in China by CTPS

ISBN 978 1 406216 89 9 (hardback)
15 14 13 12 11
10 9 8 7 6 5 4 3 2 1

ISBN 978 1 406219 74 6 (paperback)
16 15 14 13 12
10 9 8 7 6 5 4 3 2 1

British Library Cataloguing in Publication Data
Tagliaferro, Linda.
The world's smartest machines. -- (Extreme machines)
629'.046-dc22
A full catalogue record for this book is available from the British Library.

Acknowledgments
We would like to thank the following for permission to reproduce photographs: Alamy p. **10** (FRANCIS JOSEPH DEAN / DEAN PICTURES); Department of Defense p. **20** (Sgt. Roberto Di Giovine, U.S. Army); Getty Images pp. **7** (Junko Kimura), **11** (AFP), **12** (Junko Kimura), **13** (Junko Kimura), **14** (AFP/KAZUHIRO NOGI), **15** (AFP/KAZUHIRO NOGI), **19** (Robert Nickelsberg), **23** (Erik Simonsen), **24** (Ethan Miller), **25** (Ethan Miller); istockphoto p. **6** (© Martin Strmko); Landov pp. **18** (ZHANG AILIN/Xinhua), **5** (REUTERS/Thaier al-Sudani); NASA pp. **26** (/JPL/Cornell University), **27**; U.S. Air Force Photo pp. **4** (Senior Airman Vernon Young), **21** bottom (Staff Sgt. Jacob N. Bailey); U.S. Army p. **21** top (Sgt. Brandon Little); U.S. Air Force photo p. **22** (Staff Sgt. Bennie J. Davis III); U.S. Navy p. **9** (John F. Williams); Volvo pp. **16**, **17**; WHOI p. **8**.

Cover photograph of NASA testing Mars Rover in new "Marscape" reproduced with the permission of NASA (JPL).

Every effort has been made to contact copyright holders of any material reproduced in this book. Any omissions will be rectified in subsequent printings if notice is given to the publisher.

Some words are shown in bold, **like this**. You can find out what they mean by looking in the glossary.

Learn more about these smart machines on page 18!

Exploring the oceans

Vehicles that move underwater help scientists learn about what lives on the ocean floor. Ships drop these special underwater vehicles into the sea. No one is inside. The vehicles take photos and make maps of the ocean floor.

Underwater vehicles take photos of the ocean floor.

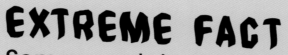

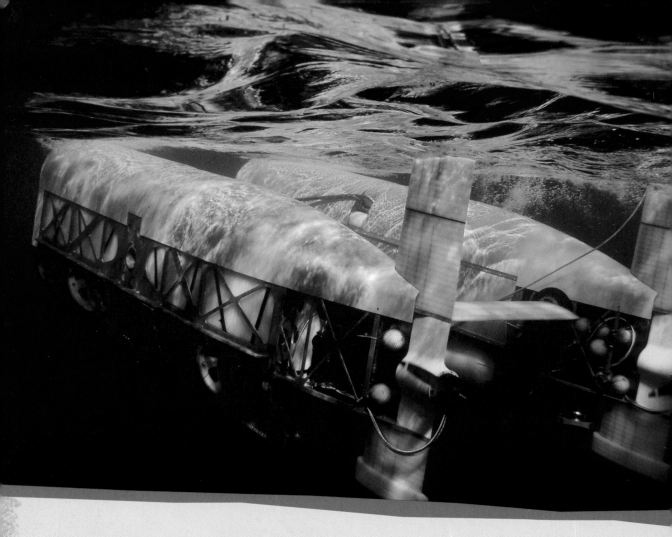

Nereus is a diving robot. Its camera sends videos of the ocean floor to scientists. The videos go through a thin wire to computers on a ship. Nereus also has an arm that collects rocks underwater.

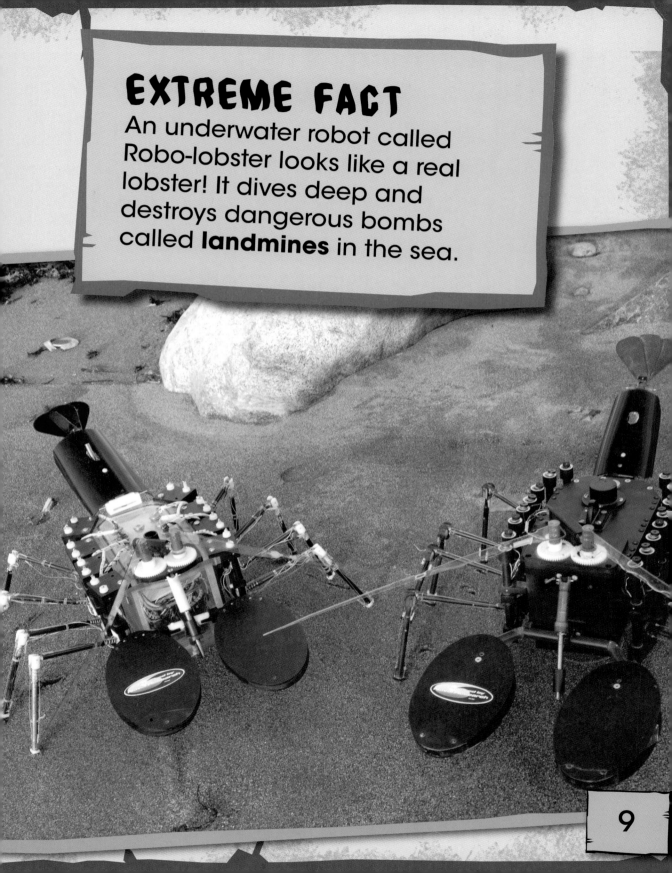

EXTREME FACT

An underwater robot called Robo-lobster looks like a real lobster! It dives deep and destroys dangerous bombs called **landmines** in the sea.

Trains without drivers

A driver usually drives a train from one station to the next. But smart trains don't need drivers. Computers inside the train pick up signals that tell it where to go. Computers tell the train when to start and stop.

No driver inside!

EXTREME FACT
Trains without drivers are safer than normal trains!

5035

11

Smart cars

Drink driving causes many accidents. The Nissan Fuga car can help stop these accidents. **Sensors** in the car know when a drunk driver gets behind the steering wheel. Then the car shuts down. It talks to the person. It tells them they cannot drive.

gear stick

EXTREME FACT

The Fuga can also tell when a driver is sleepy. It tells the driver to stop and have a rest!

The Nissan Pivo 2 is a car that wants you to be happy. When you drive it, a robotic face watches you. It also listens to your voice. If you don't seem happy, it tries to cheer you up. It talks to you and nods its head.

robotic face

NISSAN

15

Sometimes drivers don't notice everything around them. This can be very dangerous. Volvo makes a car that can help prevent accidents. **Lasers** and **radar** sense when other cars are too close. Then the Volvo quickly puts its brakes on to stop a crash.

This car of the future can watch the road for you!

Danger ahead!

Soldiers and the police sometimes have to look for bombs. But many bombs are too dangerous for people to touch. Special machines are controlled from far away, like remote controlled toy cars. These machines have cameras. They can "see" at night.

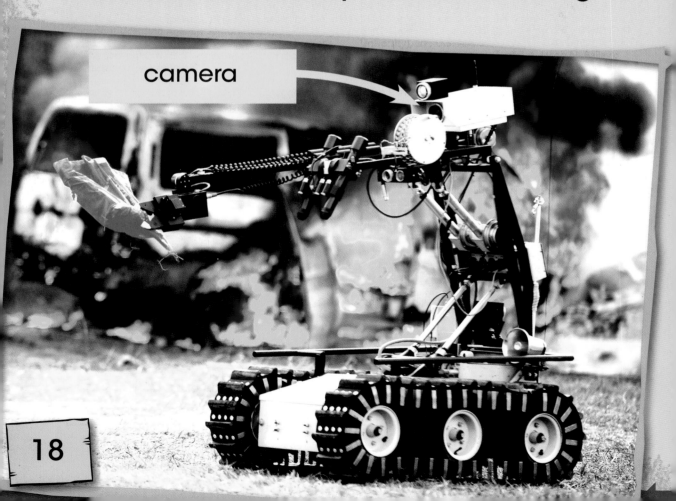

camera

arm

These machines have arms that carry bombs far away.

19

Built for battle

Apache helicopters are powerful aircraft. They use radar to find targets. Apaches do not show up on enemy radar screens. They can fly low and hide from enemies.

the pilot looks here

EXTREME FACT

At night, computers send pictures of what is below to a small display on the pilot's helmet. Then the pilot can "see" targets in the dark!

Hiding in the sky

Countries at war often send planes to attack enemies. On the ground, **radar** can sense enemy planes above. But **stealth bombers** are different. They can't be seen on radar screens. They use smart controls to make sure their bombs hit enemy targets.

EXTREME FACT
Stealth bombers look unusual. Some look like giant wings. Others have no tail.

23

Planes without pilots

Drones are planes that fly without pilots. Someone on the ground operates the drone. The controls look like a big computer game. The operator moves a joystick. Drones take videos to send back to ground control. They shoot missiles to destroy enemies.

joystick

Alone on Mars

No human has ever been to Mars. But Mars **Rovers** can explore there. Scientists on Earth control where the Rovers go. The Rovers study the dust on Mars. They tell scientists what types of rocks are there. Cameras send pictures of Mars back to Earth.

Mars Rover's camera

This is Mars as
seen from a Rover.

Test yourself!

Match the smart machines with what they do:

① Apache helicopter

② Nereus

③ Robo-lobster

④ Mars Rover

⑤ Nissan Fuga

a This machine studies the dust on Mars.

b Its computers tell pilots what aircraft is on the ground.

c This machine collects rocks underwater.

d This robot looks like a sea creature.

e This machine knows when someone is too tired to drive.

Glossary

drone an aeroplane without a pilot inside

inventors people who think of and create new things

landmine a bomb hidden in the ground

laser a special beam of light

radar a machine that can tell where aeroplanes are flying

rovers machines on wheels that travel without drivers

sensor part of a machine that picks up information

signal a word or an action that gives a message to people or machines

stealth bomber aeroplane that cannot be found by radar

vehicle machine that moves people or things